FAMOUS PEOPLE
FAMOUS LIVES

Biographies of famous people to
support the curriculum.

Martin Luther King

by Verna Wilkins

Illustrations by Lynne Willey

W

FRANKLIN WATTS

NEW YORK•LONDON•SYDNEY

First published in 1998 by
Franklin Watts
96 Leonard Street
London
EC2A 4RH

Franklin Watts Australia
14 Mars Road
Lane Cove
NSW 2066

ISBN: 0 7496 2983 5

A CIP catalogue record for this book
is available from the British Library.

Dewey Decimal Classification Number: 323

10 9 8 7 6 5 4 3

Series editor: Sarah Ridley
Series designer: Kirstie Billingham
Consultant: Dr Anne Millard

Printed in Great Britain

Martin Luther King

On a Saturday morning in 1929,
Martin Luther King was born
in the south of the United States
of America. He had a brother
and a sister and his family was
quite wealthy.

One day, when he was six, Martin went out to play at his friend's house. His friend's mother looked at him strangely and said to him, "You boys are old enough for school now – you can't play here any more. Go away."

Martin was very upset and
ran home.

"Why," he asked his mother, "can't I play with my friend any more?"

His mother held him close and explained. "Some white people are made to think that they are better than black people. You are as good as anyone else, and don't you ever forget that."

Martin began to notice signs
that read, "No Colored Allowed.
Whites only."

He learned from his parents that
those signs meant that black
children had to go to schools
that were shabby. They meant
that black people could not eat
where white people ate.

He learned also that black people
had to sit at the back of the bus.

One day, on a shopping trip,
he raced to a lift. It had beautiful
shiny buttons he could push.

"Let's use this one," he said to
his mother.

WHITES LIFT

"Shush," she said to him. "This one is not for us. We must use that one."

She pointed to an ugly, old lift. This made Martin unhappy.

COLORED LIFT

Martin's parents sent him to a good school. He was very clever and finished school three years earlier than was usual.

Then he went to university.
He made many good friends
there and worked hard. He also
loved clothes!

One summer, he took a holiday job in a northern city, a long way from home. Here there were no signs saying, "Whites Only, No Colored." Martin felt happy. He decided then that he wanted black people to be treated the same as white people, all over America.

He decided to become a preacher when he left university. In church, he would preach for a change in the laws.

After he had passed his first degree, Martin went on to study religion. He also thought about ways to change the unfair laws against black people.

In 1951, Martin graduated from college with the highest grades in his year. His parents gave him a brand new car. He was delighted.

Then Martin fell in love with a music student. He married Coretta when he was twenty-four years old.

He still continued his studies.

In 1955, he was awarded a
special degree, called a Doctorate
in Theology, and became
Dr. Martin Luther King.

Now that he had finished his studies, Martin became a minister of a church. As he had planned, he preached and prayed about the unfair laws against black people. He and thousands of others marched against these bad laws.

Eventually, one law was changed so that black children and white children could go to the same schools. Martin was pleased with this success. But there was more to be done.

COLORED PASSENGERS

Then, not long afterwards, a
woman called Rosa Parks was
on her way home from work.
She climbed onto a bus and sat
down in the black section.

22

When the bus was full, the driver ordered the black people to stand so that the whites could sit down. Rosa Parks refused and the police arrested her.

Rosa was found guilty and fined, even though she had done nothing wrong. This made many black people angry. Martin saw a chance to organise black people to change this law.

So black people refused to use the buses. Some shared cars to get to work, and some walked everywhere. The white people who owned the buses lost lots of money.

Eventually, almost a year later, the law was changed and black people could use the buses in the same way as whites could.

Still, Martin continued to preach against bad laws. By 1957, the whole world had begun to take an interest in his work. He led many marches of black people fighting for better rights in America.

He was arrested over one hundred times for his part in the marches.

By now, Coretta and Martin had four children and the family moved back to the town where Martin was born. Here Martin preached at his father's church and enjoyed spending time with his family.

He continued to organise protest marches, because there was so much more to be done.

Even though some laws had
been changed, black people
were still being treated unfairly.
This made Martin very sad.

So, Martin continued to organise marches. Sometimes he was arrested on these marches and once he was locked in a dark cell by himself for nine days.

Eventually, even young children joined the protests. A large group of them marched against the laws stopping black people from using some restaurants, libraries and toilets.

The police ordered powerful
hoses to be turned on them and
many were hurt. Some politicians
were horrified at how events
were turning out. So, ninety days
later, the laws were changed.

Still there was more to be done. In the summer of 1963, a huge number of people, both black and white, marched peacefully in Washington. It was on this day that Martin Luther King gave his famous speech.

"I have a dream," he said, "that my four children will one day live in a nation where they will be judged, not by the colour of their skin, but by the content of their character..."

I have a dream...

Around this time, Martin received a series of letters saying, "You will be killed."

"I don't think I'm going to live to forty," he told Coretta, his wife. They were worried. Change was so slow.

However, there was some good news soon after as Martin was awarded the Nobel Peace Prize. He felt encouraged and continued his difficult task.

Daily News

Martin Luther King wins Nobel Peace Prize.

Martin then began his next campaign. Very few black people were registered to vote in elections. "You must register to vote," he begged them. "That way black people will be able to influence the government more."

Martin and his supporters organised even more marches. Many times they were stopped by police. And many times violence erupted.

By this time, more white people were joining the marchers. They realised that America needed to change. Some white people were attacked for joining the black marchers. Sometimes policemen tried to stop the marchers by force.

END SEGREGATE RULES IN PUBLIC SCHOOL

VOTING RIGHTS NOW

As a result of all the work done by Martin Luther King and his followers, the Voting Rights Act was passed in 1965. At last black people had the right to vote. Martin Luther King was in the capital to witness the occasion.

In April 1968, Martin Luther King travelled with friends to Memphis, Tennessee. Here, he spoke to two thousand followers. He spoke peacefully. "I have a dream," he said, "... that the brotherhood of man will become a reality..."

After this successful day, Martin was relaxing on the balcony of his hotel before dinner. Suddenly someone shot him. His friends rushed him to hospital but doctors could not save his life.

Further Facts

Martin Luther King Day

As Martin was such a powerful leader, who achieved so much good, he is remembered every year with a public holiday in America. His life is celebrated on the third Monday in January.

Martin Luther King Foundation

This organisation aims through education to continue Martin's fight against racism. As Martin said, "Together we must learn to live as brothers/sisters or together we will be forced to perish as fools."

Who killed Martin Luther King?

James Earl Ray was found guilty of the murder of Martin Luther King. He was sentenced to ninety-nine years in prison. However, he now claims that he is innocent and has blamed another man. It is said that he has been visited in prison by relatives of Martin Luther King who believe his story.

Some important dates in Martin Luther King's lifetime

1929   Martin Luther King is born in Atlanta, Georgia, USA.

1948   Martin gains his first degree in Sociology.

1951   Martin studies at seminary college.

1953   Coretta Scott and Martin Luther King get married.

1954   Martin becomes pastor of a church in Atlanta.

1955   Boston University awards Martin his Doctorate in Theology.

1955   Martin organises marches to highlight the case of Rosa Parks.

1958   Martin finishes his first book, 'Stride toward Freedom'.

1960   Martin moves to the Ebenezer Baptist Church where he preaches with his father.

1961-3   Martin fights many campaigns to improve life for black people in the USA.

1963   Before a crowd of 200,000 people, Martin gives his 'I have a dream' speech.

1964   Martin awarded Nobel Peace Prize.

1965   The Voting Rights Act is passed as a result of all the hard work of Martin and his supporters.

1968   Martin is shot dead on April 4th.